GENEROSITY

Responding to God's Radical Grace in Community

LeAnn Baker

GENEROSITY

Responding to God's Radical Grace in Community

A Seven-Session Study Guide by
Redeemer Presbyterian Church | gospel in life

Generosity: Responding to God's Radical Grace in Community
A Seven-Session Study Guide from Redeemer Presbyterian Church

Copyright © 2016 by Redeemer Presbyterian Church, located at 1166 Avenue of the Americas, 16th floor, New York, NY 10036.

Previously used at Redeemer Presbyterian Church under the title "Generosity: Studies from the Gospel of Luke."

ISBN-13: 978-1-944549-00-8

Generosity: Responding to God's Radical Grace in Community was written and developed by the staff of Redeemer Presbyterian Church of New York City.

Cover and interior design: Lee Marcum

Printed in the United States of America

Second Printing — September 2016

CONTENTS

INTRODUCTION

In the fall of 2012, Dr. Timothy Keller and the pastors at Redeemer Presbyterian Church preached a series of sermons on the theme of gospel-driven generosity. This Bible study was developed by the church staff to accompany the weekly sermon series.

What is gospel-driven generosity? It's a theme that is pervasive throughout Scripture, but which we so often reduce to a legalistic requirement or an obligatory task. We hope this study will help you consider the different aspects of generosity—from hospitality to financial giving to forgiveness—as joyful responses to God's grace towards us.

Each study will take you through four main ideas:

1. *The Text.* What is the main point of the Scripture passage?

2. *The Text in the Bigger Story.* How does this text connect to the larger narrative of the Bible?

3. *Jesus Completing the Story.* How does this text culminate in the life and work of Jesus?

4. *Living Out the Story.* How does this text move us, in practical ways, toward greater faith and repentance?

Keep these in mind as you go through each passage and process them as a group. There are additional notes to guide discussion leaders at the back.

Finally, as your group studies the Bible together, it is helpful to remember that since all Scripture is revelation about God and Jesus Christ is the culmination of this, then fundamentally all Scripture (both Old Testament and New Testament) is about him—his life, death and resurrection (Luke 24:27, 45-47).

Generosity and God's Grace

SCRIPTURE

Luke 18:9-17 (NIV)

⁹ To some who were confident of their own righteousness and looked down on everybody else, Jesus told this parable: ¹⁰ "Two men went up to the temple to pray, one a Pharisee and the other a tax collector. ¹¹ The Pharisee stood up and prayed about himself: 'God, I thank you that I am not like other men—robbers, evildoers, adulterers—or even like this tax collector. ¹² I fast twice a week and give a tenth of all I get.'

¹³ "But the tax collector stood at a distance. He would not even look up to heaven, but beat his breast and said, 'God, have mercy on me, a sinner.'

¹⁴ "I tell you that this man, rather than the other, went home justified before God. For everyone who exalts himself will be humbled, and he who humbles himself will be exalted."

¹⁵ People were also bringing babies to Jesus to have him touch them. When the disciples saw this, they rebuked them. ¹⁶ But Jesus called the children to him and said, "Let the little children come to me, and do not hinder them, for the kingdom of God belongs to such as these.

¹⁷ I tell you the truth, anyone who will not receive the kingdom of God like a little child will never enter it."

DISCUSSION

Goal of This Study: To understand that God accepts those who humbly receive his mercy, not those who believe they can earn it. From this distinct paradigm we receive the theological foundation for generous living. To the extent we are humbled by our unworthiness as recipients of God's grace will we be agents of life-giving, generous grace to those around us.

Background Information: Though Luke does not specify that Jesus' audience was Pharisees, his description of "some who were confident of their own righteousness" would lead us to assume a Pharisee-heavy audience. In this parable, Jesus contrasts two praying men, presumably two fellow believers. The contrast is not between an unbeliever and a believer, for both men pray and worship God. Rather, Jesus takes pains to show that the great division in the human race is not between the moral and the immoral, or even between the religious and the irreligious—it is between the spiritually humble and the proudly self-sufficient. The proudly self-sufficient include people who think they can get along just fine without God (or certainly without a God who tells them what to do!), so it encompasses what we would call the skeptic or the secular person. But—and here is the shocking part of the parable—it also includes many who are very religious, highly moral, and even those who believe the Bible word for word.

The Text

1. Jesus describes two men who went up to the temple to pray. What do the two men have in common? How do they differ?

They both came to pray.

Their understanding of Gods grace were far apart,

2. **What do their prayers tell us about both their view of God and what they believe is acceptable to him?**

3. **What do the Pharisee and Jesus' disciples (vv. 15-17) have in common? How do they regard others of lower status?**

The Text in the Bigger Story

Read Micah 6:6-8

⁶ With what shall I come before the LORD
    and bow down before the exalted God?
  Shall I come before him with burnt offerings,
    with calves a year old?
⁷ Will the LORD be pleased with thousands of rams,
    with ten thousand rivers of oil?
  Shall I offer my firstborn for my transgression,
    the fruit of my body for the sin of my soul?
⁸ He has showed you, O man, what is good.
    And what does the LORD require of you?
  To act justly and to love mercy
    and to walk humbly with your God.

4. The Pharisee considered himself great because of his tithes and fasts, but in the Micah text we see that even the most extraordinary works are insufficient for meeting God's demands. What did the Pharisee and the readers of Micah fail to grasp about what God truly desires? What does this say about our efforts to earn God's approval?

Jesus Completing the Story

5. What do we learn from this parable about the necessity of Jesus' sacrifice for sin? How does his voluntary humility change our posture toward God?

Living Out the Story

6. To which of the men do you more readily relate? Why?

7. What are some of the "good deeds" you rely on to earn God's favor?

8. How does the experience of God's graciousness and generosity to us, shown in the sacrifice of Jesus, radically alter our motivation for good deeds?

PRAYER

Pray together (aloud or silently) through the following items related to today's study:

○ *Praise* God that it is his good pleasure to reveal his kingdom to "little children," those who are humble and poor in spirit (Matthew 5:3, 11:25-26). Praise him for Jesus, who humbled himself and became obedient to death on the cross, in order to share with us his resurrection and exaltation.

○ *Confess* our tendency to be self-reliant and proud, which closes us off to receiving God's grace. Confess how easily we look down on those we deem insignificant and treat them with contempt, rather than compassion.

❍ *Ask* God to reveal those areas in our lives where we do not depend on him or recognize his graciousness to us. Ask that he would show us our dependence of the idols of self, security, accomplishments, and acumen; pray for spiritual insight to recognize how flimsy and empty these idols are. Pray for humbled, repentant hearts that turn to him for grace and experience his compassion.

Generosity and Relationships

SCRIPTURE

Luke 17:3-10 (NIV)

³ So watch yourselves. "If your brother sins, rebuke him, and if he repents, forgive him. ⁴ If he sins against you seven times in a day, and seven times comes back to you and says, 'I repent,' forgive him."

⁵ The apostles said to the Lord, "Increase our faith!"

⁶ He replied, "If you have faith as small as a mustard seed, you can say to this mulberry tree, 'Be uprooted and planted in the sea,' and it will obey you.

⁷ "Suppose one of you had a servant plowing or looking after the sheep. Would he say to the servant when he comes in from the field, 'Come along now and sit down to eat'? ⁸ Would he not rather say, 'Prepare my supper, get yourself ready and wait on me while I eat and drink; after that you may eat and drink'? ⁹ Would he thank the servant because he did what he was told to do? ¹⁰ So you also, when you have done everything you were told to do, should say, 'We are unworthy servants; we have only done our duty.'"

DISCUSSION

Goal of This Study: To understand that in Christ we receive forgiveness for sins, which enables us to be generous in our relationships and forgive others without limit.

Background Information: Generosity means living for God and others, not for ourselves. It embodies a lifestyle shaped by a deep conviction that in Christ we find true riches and abounding treasure. Generous people do not use others for personal gain, demand that their rights be upheld at all costs, or hold grudges against those who offend them. Instead, the gospel changes their attitudes toward others so that they are able to constantly wipe the slate clean and eliminate all record of wrongs. Generous people cancel debts and absorb the cost themselves. In the above passage, Jesus makes it clear to his disciples who they really are— servants whose extraordinary debt to God, their master, has been forgiven. As a result of experiencing such forgiveness, the appropriate response is to seek reconciliation with those who wrong them.

The Text

1. What is your response to being called an "unworthy servant," whose duty it is to offer unlimited forgiveness?

2. What is the connection between Jesus' teaching on forgiveness (vv. 3-4) and his response to his disciples about faith and duty (vv. 6-10)?

3. What are the specific steps listed in Jesus' command to forgive and how is this different from the ways we have thought of forgiveness?

The Text in the Bigger Story

Commentators note that Jesus is referring to Leviticus 19:17-18.

[17] "Do not hate your brother in your heart. Rebuke your neighbor frankly so you will not share in his guilt. [18] Do not seek revenge or bear a grudge against one of your people, but love your neighbor as yourself. I am the LORD."

4. What do you think it means to "rebuke your neighbor frankly" in the context of loving your neighbor as yourself?

Jesus Completing the Story

5. Jesus came "not to be served, but to serve and to give his life as a ransom for many" (Matthew 20:28). How does Jesus' life as a servant transform your understanding of what it means to forgive?

Living Out the Story

6. How does the forgiveness God offers us through Jesus radically transform the way we extend forgiveness to others?

7. We are called to be a people of reconciliation and peace, yet we often find ourselves in situations where a lack of forgiveness has alienated us from those who have wronged us. What are some practical steps we can take to reach out to those who have sinned against us?

PRAYER

Pray together (aloud or silently) through the following items related to the study:

○ *Praise* God for his endless forgiveness and radical kindness toward us. Praise Jesus that he humbled himself and became a lowly servant who gave himself for our salvation, that we might share with him the riches of God's inheritance.

○ *Confess* that our hearts are often hard toward one another and that we too often forget the grace that has been lavished on us. Confess that we are prone to hold grudges against others, disobeying Jesus' command to freely forgive.

○ *Ask* that God would open our eyes to his grace and mercy and that by beholding his grace to us, we would readily forgive others and diligently seek reconciliation for broken relationships. Pray that as he helps us understand Jesus' humility and service, that we also would humble ourselves and be generous in how we relate to others, especially those who wrong us.

Hospitality and God's Grace

SCRIPTURE

Luke 14:12-24 (NIV)

¹² Then Jesus said to his host, "When you give a luncheon or dinner, do not invite your friends, your brothers or relatives, or your rich neighbors; if you do, they may invite you back and so you will be repaid. ¹³ But when you give a banquet, invite the poor, the crippled, the lame, the blind, ¹⁴ and you will be blessed. Although they cannot repay you, you will be repaid at the resurrection of the righteous."

¹⁵ When one of those at the table with him heard this, he said to Jesus, "Blessed is the man who will eat at the feast in the kingdom of God."

¹⁶ Jesus replied: "A certain man was preparing a great banquet and invited many guests. ¹⁷ At the time of the banquet he sent his servant to tell those who had been invited, 'Come, for everything is now ready.'

¹⁸ "But they all alike began to make excuses. The first said, 'I have just bought a field, and I must go and see it. Please excuse me.'

¹⁹ "Another said, 'I have just bought five yoke of oxen, and I'm on my way to try them out. Please excuse me.'

²⁰ "Still another said, 'I just got married, so I can't come.'

[21] "The servant came back and reported this to his master. Then the owner of the house became angry and ordered his servant, 'Go out quickly into the streets and alleys of the town and bring in the poor, the crippled, the blind and the lame.'

[22] "'Sir,' the servant said, 'what you ordered has been done, but there is still room.'

[23] "Then the master told his servant, 'Go out to the roads and country lanes and make them come in, so that my house will be full. [24] I tell you, not one of those men who were invited will get a taste of my banquet.'"

DISCUSSION

Goal of This Study: To understand our position as unworthy guests welcomed into God's kingdom and to likewise extend hospitality to others without expecting repayment.

Background Information: In Jesus' time there was no organized welfare system. Wealthy people in the community were expected to help neighbors who had economic problems. But this system was not in any way rooted in compassion for the poor and marginalized; rather, it was based on a system of self-interest. When the wealthy aided the poor, it was done with great fanfare as a sign of their status in the community. In the same way, when those with resources showed generosity and hospitality, the acts were done with the expectation that the favor be returned in the form of political preferences, economic breaks, and public acknowledgement.

Jesus' teaching was radically different. When he told the parable of a man who planned a great banquet, he was portraying a typical way a wealthy man sought to sustain and create new relationships with those who received his patronage. In the parable, the host discovered that the expected guests turned down his invitation. Instead, his invitation was accepted by those who couldn't begin to repay it.

Jesus is revealing the tendency of the religious and self-sufficient to resist the gospel, while the needy tend to embrace it. In doing so, he calls his followers to extend hospitality in a way that defies the patronage system of the day and provides for those who have nothing to offer in return.

The Text

1. Who are the people you are most likely to invite to a party?

> Friends & Family
> I've had church friends.

2. In verses 15-24, two different groups of people are invited to a great banquet at two different times. How would you describe the first group that was invited to the banquet?

> They had everything they needed meaning (well off.)
> They didn't need to be around the crowd.

3. How would you describe the second group that was invited to the banquet?

> They were crippled, poor lame & blind needing help from others,
> They were outcast, overlooked by wealthy people

The Text in the Bigger Story

Jesus' contemporaries would have been reminded of the future kingdom banquet of Isaiah 25:6-9.

> "⁶ On this mountain the Lord Almighty will prepare
>   a feast of rich food for all peoples,
> a banquet of aged wine—
>   the best of meats and the finest of wines.
> ⁷ On this mountain he will destroy
>   the shroud that enfolds all peoples,
> the sheet that covers all nations;
>   he will swallow up death forever.
> The Sovereign LORD will wipe away the tears
>   from all faces;
> he will remove the disgrace of his people
>   from all the earth.
> The LORD has spoken.
>
> ⁹ In that day they will say,
>   "Surely this is our God;
>   we trusted in him, and he saved us.
> This is the LORD, we trusted in him;
>   let us rejoice and be glad in his salvation."

4. How would you describe the Isaiah feast, and what does this tell you about God and his kingdom?

A great feast for all, nothing but the best. Enough for all,

Jesus Completing the Story

5. What do you learn from this parable about the heart and intention of God?

Gods promess to provide in Love
Eternal Kingdom with Joy &
Celebration - were saved from sin theirs
no shame its forgiven - no suffering
That were made hole.

Living Out the Story

6. Who are the people on the margins of the Luke banquet? And who are the people on the margins of our invitation lists?

Rich not needing anything

Should be people who haven't much & need help & loved

7. The Greek word for hospitality is *philoxenia*, which literally means "love of strangers." What are some ways that we can make room for those who are not typical "party invitees," those who are unwelcomed and excluded in our society?

We can envite them to a meal at our homes To get to know them better.

PRAYER

Pray together (aloud or silently) through the following items related to the study:

○ **Praise** God for inviting us to his lavish, eternal kingdom feast. Praise God that we do not have to rely on how much money we give, how many hours we serve, or how we measure up to his moral code, but only on the generous sacrifice of Jesus Christ on our behalf.

○ **Confess** that we forget how free and lavish his grace is toward us. Confess that we have not been truly generous with others, often expecting something in return for our hospitality or generosity.

○ **Ask** for a deeper understanding and experience of the gospel message, which tells us that God extended hospitality to us even when we had no means to return the favor. Ask that this would cause us to show a no-strings-attached kind of grace to others, particularly those on the margins of our society.

Generosity and Ministry

SCRIPTURE

Luke 9:49-10:2 (NIV)

[49] "Master," said John, "we saw a man driving out demons in your name and we tried to stop him, because he is not one of us."

[50] "Do not stop him," Jesus said, "for whoever is not against you is for you."

[51] As the time approached for him to be taken up to heaven, Jesus resolutely set out for Jerusalem. [52] And he sent messengers on ahead, who went into a Samaritan village to get things ready for him; [53] but the people there did not welcome him, because he was heading for Jerusalem. [54] When the disciples James and John saw this, they asked, "Lord, do you want us to call fire down from heaven to destroy them?" [55] But Jesus turned and rebuked them, [56] and they went to another village.

[57] As they were walking along the road, a man said to him, "I will follow you wherever you go."

[58] Jesus replied, "Foxes have holes and birds of the air have nests, but the Son of Man has no place to lay his head."

[59] He said to another man, "Follow me." But the man replied, "Lord, first let me go and bury my father."

[60] Jesus said to him, "Let the dead bury their own dead, but you go and proclaim the kingdom of God."

[61] Still another said, "I will follow you, Lord; but first let me go back and say good-bye to my family."

[62] Jesus replied, "No one who puts his hand to the plow and looks back is fit for service in the kingdom of God."

[1] After this the Lord appointed seventy-two others and sent them two by two ahead of him to every town and place where he was about to go. [2] He told them, "The harvest is plentiful, but the workers are few. Ask the Lord of the harvest, therefore, to send out workers into his harvest field."

DISCUSSION

Goal of This Study: To see that Jesus, by giving up his own life for us, empowers us to give all of ourselves in service to him and to others.

Background Information: As Jesus' disciples, we are called to live generously and serve others. We are called to be compassionate toward others because God showed compassion toward us in Jesus' sacrifice on our behalf. If we lose our footing on this foundation of grace—if we miss the grace of God, as Hebrews 12:15 exhorts us not to—then we become vulnerable to bitterness and other troubles. For example, if we believe that God shows his favor toward us because of our level of commitment to him or to church activities, we might become judgmental and condescending to those who we consider to be less committed. We might think: "I work extremely hard on behalf of the church or such-and-such ministry—so you should too! And if you don't work as hard as I do, you are undeserving!" This self-righteous approach is contrary to what it means to follow Jesus. The gospel does not allow us to think this way. The gospel tells us that we were saved in spite of not living right and not obeying as we should. We follow Jesus out of deep gratitude for his grace. We may be saddened when we see others disobey. We may even speak directly to them with truth and grace. Truly grasping God's grace dissolves all sense of self-righteousness; we realize that no one is accepted by God because of what he or she has done, but only by grace alone. So it is through the love and kindness of God that we are sent out to do the work of Jesus.

The Text

1. **Before sending his followers out to serve others, Jesus first clears up misconceptions about what it means to follow him. What are some modern-day misconceptions you have heard about what it means to follow Jesus?**

   Judge mental

2. **What were the misconceptions of Jesus' listeners (vv. 49-62)?**

   mark 9 -
   casting out

3. **What do you learn from Jesus' response?**

The Text in the Bigger Story

In 2 Corinthians 5:17-20, the Apostle Paul further unpacks this idea that Jesus' followers are sent out into the world to serve.

[17] "Therefore, if anyone is in Christ, he is a new creation; the old has gone, the new has come! [18] All this is from God, who reconciled us to himself through Christ and gave us the ministry of reconciliation: [19] that God was reconciling the world to himself in Christ, not counting men's sins against them. And he has committed to us the message of reconciliation. [20] We are therefore Christ's ambassadors, as though God were making his appeal through us. We implore you on Christ's behalf: Be reconciled to God."

4. What are the primary responsibilities of an ambassador, and what should be our responsibilities as "Christ's ambassadors"?

peace a goodwill To All, we are messengers to share his love to others, and people should see Jesus' love in us,

5. What are some challenges to our roles as Christ's ambassadors?

1, 2, 3

Helping others

Jesus Completing the Story

6. What about Jesus' life and death helps us understand his rebuke in verses 49-62?

Jesus gave his whole life to save us from our sins.

Living Out the Story

7. In verse 2 Jesus tells his followers that "the harvest is plentiful, but the workers are few." In what areas of your community or neighborhood do you see plentiful needs with few workers?

8. What prejudices do we harbor in our own hearts and what steps can we take to seek reconciliation?

PRAYER

Pray together (aloud or silently) through the following items related to the study:

○ **Praise** God for his generosity to us, that although we were his enemies, he showed us compassion and reconciliation. Praise him that he laid down the riches of heaven to invite us into his kingdom. Praise him that he reconciled us to himself.

○ **Thank** him for including us in his work of gospel reconciliation.

○ **Confess** our prejudices against others, which prevent us from serving them. Confess our busyness and our tendency to elevate secondary things over God's kingdom.

○ **Ask** that God would be the primary focus of our entire beings and that he would change any haughty and disdainful attitudes toward others that may reside in our hearts. Ask that we would be faithful witnesses of his message of reconciliation to all those we meet.

STUDY #5

Generosity and Wealth, Part 1

SCRIPTURE

Luke 18:18-30 (NIV)

[18] A certain ruler asked him, "Good teacher, what must I do to inherit eternal life?"

[19] "Why do you call me good?" Jesus answered. "No one is good—except God alone. [20] You know the commandments: 'Do not commit adultery, do not murder, do not steal, do not give false testimony, honor your father and mother.'"

[21] "All these I have kept since I was a boy," he said.

[22] When Jesus heard this, he said to him, "You still lack one thing. Sell everything you have and give to the poor, and you will have treasure in heaven. Then come, follow me."

[23] When he heard this, he became very sad, because he was a man of great wealth. [24] Jesus looked at him and said, "How hard it is for the rich to enter the kingdom of God! [25] Indeed, it is easier for a camel to go through the eye of a needle than for a rich man to enter the kingdom of God."

[26] Those who heard this asked, "Who then can be saved?" [27] Jesus replied, "What is impossible with men is possible with God." [28] Peter said to him, "We have left all we had to follow you!"

[29] "I tell you the truth," Jesus said to them, "no one who has left home or wife or brothers or parents or children for the sake of the

kingdom of God [30] will fail to receive many times as much in this age and, in the age to come, eternal life."

DISCUSSION

Goal of This Study: To see the value of true wealth and understand how God's radical generosity to us transforms the way we regard everything we own.

Background Information: In the ancient world, wealth was viewed as a sign of God's favor. The belief was that the richer you were, the more God had blessed you. As a result, wealth was often equated with holiness. But Jesus turns that way of thinking completely on its head. In this encounter with the rich ruler, he says that the richer you are, the harder it is to enter the kingdom of God. Jesus is warning about the spiritual danger of wealth that blinds people to their need of salvation. He is saying that it takes God's supernatural intervention to bring people—especially successful and financially secure people—into the kingdom.

Jesus is not only addressing wealth, but also identifying anything that could become one's functional salvation (a means of redemption that replaces God's salvation through Jesus). The call to follow Jesus does not merely require trusting him for salvation; it also demands that we stop trusting all other things for our security and self-worth. It is seeing how much more important he is than everything else. And to those who give up everything to follow him, Jesus assures them that they have not misplaced their faith. They may lose family, but they get a new family in the Christian community; they may lose some material security, but they gain a security that is rooted in God's love and faithfulness. Following Jesus, therefore, requires radical faith in his promises.

The Text

1. What are the possessions you hold most dear?

2. The rich ruler claimed that he had faithfully kept all the commandments since his youth. Why then was it so difficult for him to follow Jesus' command in verse 22?

3. Is Jesus' command to sell everything and give to the poor required of everyone who seeks to follow him? Why or why not?

4. What are some of the things in which we place our trust and security? And why are these things such spiritual traps?

The Text In The Bigger Story

The rich ruler thought he had done everything he was required to do because he kept the Ten Commandments. In Deuteronomy 10:12-15, however, God showed his people what true obedience meant.

[12] And now, Israel, what does the LORD your God ask of you but to fear the LORD your God, to walk in obedience to him, to love him, to serve the LORD your God with all your heart and with all your soul, [13] and to observe the LORD's commands and decrees that I am giving you today for your own good?

[14] To the LORD your God belong the heavens, even the highest heavens, the earth and everything in it. [15] Yet the LORD set his affection on your ancestors and loved them, and he chose you, their descendants, above all the nations—as it is today.

5. According to this passage, what was lacking about the rich ruler's obedience?

Jesus Completing the Story

6. Jesus says that no one who has forsaken family or riches to follow him "will fail to receive many times as much in this age and, in the age to come, eternal life." What are some things we find in Jesus that our idols cannot provide?

Living Out the Story

7. What would it look like to faithfully serve God with our wealth and all he has given us? What area of your life would be most affected?

PRAYER

Pray together (aloud or silently) through the following items related to the study:

⊙ *Praise* God that he provides a way for all people to enter his kingdom through his son, Jesus. Praise him that we are heirs to the treasures of heaven, which far exceeds anything we experience in this world.

⊙ *Confess* that we make idols of the blessings God gives us, particularly our money and our time. Confess that we are tight-fisted and that we are unwilling to offer unto God what is rightfully his.

⊙ *Ask* for an experience of God's generosity. Ask that the treasure of knowing Jesus would become so much more real and valuable than all the worthless idols we cling to. Ask that as God begins to reign supreme in our lives, that everything we own would be used in his service and for his glory.

Generosity and Wealth, Part 2

SCRIPTURE

Luke 16:1-14 (NIV)

[1] Jesus told his disciples: "There was a rich man whose manager was accused of wasting his possessions. [2] So he called him in and asked him, 'What is this I hear about you? Give an account of your management, because you cannot be manager any longer.'

[3] "The manager said to himself, 'What shall I do now? My master is taking away my job. I'm not strong enough to dig, and I'm ashamed to beg—[4] I know what I'll do so that, when I lose my job here, people will welcome me into their houses.'

[5] "So he called in each one of his master's debtors. He asked the first, 'How much do you owe my master?'

[6] "'Eight hundred gallons of olive oil,' he replied. "The manager told him, 'Take your bill, sit down quickly, and make it four hundred.' [7] "Then he asked the second, 'And how much do you owe?' "'A thousand bushels of wheat,' he replied. "He told him, 'Take your bill and make it eight hundred.'

[8] "The master commended the dishonest manager because he had acted shrewdly. For the people of this world are more shrewd in dealing with their own kind than are the people of the light. [9] I tell you, use worldly wealth to gain friends for yourselves, so that when it is gone, you will be welcomed into eternal dwellings.

[10] "Whoever can be trusted with very little can also be trusted with much, and whoever is dishonest with very little will also be dishonest with much. [11] So if you have not been trustworthy in handling worldly wealth, who will trust you with true riches? [12] And if you have not been trustworthy with someone else's property, who will give you property of your own?

[13] "No servant can serve two masters. Either he will hate the one and love the other, or he will be devoted to the one and despise the other. You cannot serve both God and Money."

[14] The Pharisees, who loved money, heard all this and were sneering at Jesus.

DISCUSSION

Goal of This Study: To see how experiencing true riches in Christ enables us to use our wealth wisely to welcome others into God's kingdom.

Background Information: This parable is about a rich man who employed a manager, often called a steward. The Greek word *oikonomon* is literally translated "the ruler of the house." He was essentially the chief operating officer of the entire estate. He was ruler over a large amount of wealth and was charged with managing it. For the most part, he was free to use and invest his master's wealth as he saw fit, and his decisions were legally binding. A perk of the job was that he lived quite well. Yet in reality, he was a servant, since he did not own anything, and he ultimately served the interests of his master, not his own.

Jesus invokes an ancient form of lesser-to-greater reasoning, as noted by, "If this is true, then how much more…" He shows us a man who has enough sense to know it is better to give up income now to insure a safe and prosperous future. He also knows that real value is in relationships, not the money itself. If people of this world have the wisdom to use their wealth with the long-term future in view, how much more should the "people of the light"— Christians? And if the people of this world realize the importance of relationships, how much more should Christians value them?

The Text

1. Why do you think Jesus would use this example to teach his disciples how to make friends?

2. What is surprising about the way in which the manager secured his future (vv. 3-7)?

3. What is Jesus teaching his followers about wealth and relationships?

The Text In The Bigger Story

In 1 Chronicles 29:12-16, King David praises God for his provision of materials to build God's temple.

[12] Wealth and honor come from you;
you are the ruler of all things.
In your hands are strength and power
to exalt and give strength to all.
[13] Now, our God, we give you thanks,
and praise your glorious name.

[14] "But who am I, and who are my people, that we should be able to give as generously as this? Everything comes from you, and we have given you only what comes from your hand. [15] We are aliens and strangers in your sight, as were all our forefathers. Our days on earth are like a shadow, without hope.

[16] O LORD our God, as for all this abundance that we have provided for building you a temple for your Holy Name, it comes from your hand, and all of it belongs to you.

4. Compare King David and the manager in Luke, particularly their attitudes about wealth. What does King David's prayer teach us about how we should view wealth?

Jesus Completing the Story

5. What "true riches" (v. 11) does Jesus give us that worldly wealth cannot?

Living Out the Story

6. Share with the group some ways you have experienced God's riches this week. How can we use our wealth (and other resources) to build relationships that welcome others into God's kingdom?

7. What are some ways we can be more generous with our money? In particular, consider how we can limit some of our spending so we can be more flexible in our giving.

PRAYER

Pray together (aloud or silently) through the following items related to the study:

○ *Praise* God for his abundant provision. Praise him for the material and spiritual blessings in our lives, which he gives us so that we might thrive and participate in his work of drawing all people to him.

○ *Confess* that we have been irresponsible in how we spend our money. Confess that we hold too tightly to the wealth God has given us, neglecting to use it for the sake of the kingdom.

○ *Ask* that God would give us an attitude like David, who considered all things as belonging to God, his master. Ask that the ways we use our money would introduce many to the love of Christ.

STUDY #7
Generosity and Power

SCRIPTURE

Luke 19:1-9 (NIV)

[1] Jesus entered Jericho and was passing through. [2] A man was there by the name of Zacchaeus; he was a chief tax collector and was wealthy. [3] He wanted to see who Jesus was, but being a short man he could not, because of the crowd. [4] So he ran ahead and climbed a sycamore-fig tree to see him, since Jesus was coming that way.

[5] When Jesus reached the spot, he looked up and said to him, "Zacchaeus, come down immediately. I must stay at your house today." [6] So he came down at once and welcomed him gladly.

[7] All the people saw this and began to mutter, "He has gone to be the guest of a 'sinner.'"

[8] But Zacchaeus stood up and said to the Lord, "Look, Lord! Here and now I give half of my possessions to the poor, and if I have cheated anybody out of anything, I will pay back four times the amount."

[9] Jesus said to him, "Today salvation has come to this house, because this man, too, is a son of Abraham."

DISCUSSION

Goal of This Study: To see that a true encounter with Jesus transforms the way we use power—not for ourselves but to serve others.

Background information: Tax collectors like Zacchaeus were collaborators with the Roman occupying forces. Rome conquered Judea, and as a way of keeping their colonies weak and economically dependent, they levied crippling taxes. A Jew who was a tax collector was in the same position as the French who cooperated with the Nazis when they took over France during World War II. They were despised as traitors. Any Jew who became a tax collector was selling his soul for money. They were, in effect, saying, "I want to be rich even if it alienates me from my people and community." (And recall that traditional values of family and community were prized above all other cultural values at this point in Jewish history.)

It is also important to note how this text reveals the difference between the gospel and religion. Note the order of events of this narrative: Jesus initiated the invitation to Zacchaeus' home. As Western readers of this text, we are not necessarily shocked by this narrative, but the people of Jesus' day would have been stunned by this development! Hospitality in our culture does not mean what it did at that time; in that culture, to eat in someone's home was a sign of affirmation and commitment. That is why the crowd was so shocked that Jesus would eat with a man who had not repented, a man considered to be a despicable person.

The order in this text demonstrates a complete reversal from what we've come to assume about religion. Jesus did not say, "Clean up your life, and then I will come to your house." It is the other way around: Jesus first goes to Zacchaeus' house, and as a response, Zacchaeus wants to clean up his life (v. 8). Jesus was essentially saying, "I am committed to you and am coming into your life; I am loving you first." As a response, Zacchaeus no longer needed his money for his sense of worth. He received from Jesus the unconditional love and acceptance he had been seeking in wealth. The minute Zacchaeus realized that Jesus was showing him this unmerited grace, the joy hits him (v. 6) and that is what changed his life!

The Text

1. What are some things we tend to value most? How have we, like Zacchaeus, "sold out" to our careers or other cultural values?

2. What are the differences between Zacchaeus before and after his encounter with Jesus?

The Text in the Bigger Story

The apostle Paul, like Zacchaeus, experienced a life-transforming encounter with Jesus and wrote about it in Philippians 3:7-8, 13-14.

[7] But whatever was to my profit I now consider loss for the sake of Christ. [8] What is more, I consider everything a loss compared to the surpassing greatness of knowing Christ Jesus my Lord, for whose sake I have lost all things. I consider them rubbish, that I may gain Christ...[13] But one thing I do: Forgetting what is behind and straining toward what is ahead, [14] I press on toward the goal

to win the prize for which God has called me heavenward in
Christ Jesus.

3. How are Paul and Zacchaeus able to joyfully let go of things that used to be so important to them?

4. What were the most obvious changes in Zacchaeus' (and Paul's) relationships to God after encountering Jesus?

Jesus Completing the Story

5. Jesus makes a remarkable statement in verse 9 that applies to all who receive him. What does it mean for a "sinner" like Zacchaeus to become a "son of Abraham"?

Living Out the Story

6. The gospel changes everything about our lives, from our most notable strengths to our innermost motives. Can you think of subtle ways in which you wield power or influence? What would it look like to have a Zacchaeus-like transformation in your sphere of influence?

7. Zacchaeus expressed delight and satisfaction in giving away his wealth. Have you experienced a similar joy in giving away power, status, possessions, or wealth?

PRAYER

Pray together (aloud or silently) through the following items related to the study:

- **Praise** God that through Jesus, he is pleased to offer us joy and fulfillment beyond anything that this world can give. Praise Jesus that he himself is salvation and that it is through him and him alone that we are saved.

- **Confess** that our love for Jesus is often replaced by affections for things that cannot satisfy. As a result, we abuse our power and influence, using them to serve our own needs and not others'.

- **Ask** God that we would experience Jesus in such a way as to transform us into people who find our greatest delight in serving him and doing his will. Ask for more properly aligned affections. Pray that we would use our power and influence to bring blessing and flourishing into the lives of those around us.

GENEROSITY
Responding to God's Radical Grace
in Community

• LEADER'S NOTES •

INSTRUCTIONS TO LEADERS

This guide is provided only as a basic framework. The goal of each lesson is not to master the material or answer all the questions, but to grow in our knowledge of Jesus and his teachings and to develop deeper relationships with one another.

That being said, you, as the leader, should review the lesson in advance with the goal of choosing the best discussion questions for your particular group. Feel free to insert your own community-building "ice breaker" question at the start of each lesson, one that aligns itself with the key principles of the lesson and will engage your group members. Feel free to pick and choose from the menu of discussion questions the ones that are best suited for your particular group. You may also want to customize the Living Out the Story questions and prayers.

We trust that you and your group members will grow together in your knowledge of God's riches in Jesus as a result of these lessons in generosity. May your hearts be enlightened to know the "riches of his glorious inheritance" that we will one day share (Ephesians 1:18).

BACKGROUND INFORMATION

This series centers on the biblical theme of generosity. Using the well-known exhortations of Jesus found in the Gospel of Luke, this study series will unveil how the power of the gospel requires a lifestyle of generosity in response. Specifically, you will learn how the inside-out message of the gospel can transform our thinking as to the use of our time, knowledge, possessions, power, and money.

STUDY #1
Generosity and God's Grace

Luke 18:9-17
See page 7

The Text (15-20 minutes)

1. Jesus describes two men who went up to the temple to pray. What do the two men have in common? How do they differ?

Use this first question as an easy on-ramp to group discussion. Discussion should compare and contrast the two men and their prayer styles. Both men came to pray, to seek God's favor, and seem to have had habits of regular prayer. But their relationship to God and their understanding of his grace are worlds apart.

2. What do their prayers tell us about both their view of God and what they believe is acceptable to him?

The goal of this question is to understand that God only accepts those who acknowledge their complete dependence on his mercy and not those who are proud and self-sufficient.

3. What do the Pharisee and Jesus' disciples (vv. 15-17) have in common? How do they regard others of lower status?

Help participants make the connection between the disciples and the Pharisee, who both looked down on those they deemed inferior. Both the Pharisee and Jesus' disciples do not understand their own sinful conditions or need for God's mercy. "If we claim to be without sin, we deceive ourselves and the truth is not in us" (1 John 1:8).

The Text in the Bigger Story (5-10 minutes)

Read Micah 6:6-8

4. The Pharisee considered himself great because of his tithes and fasts, but in the Micah text we see that even the most extraordinary works are insufficient for meeting God's demands. What did the Pharisee and the readers of Micah fail to grasp about what God truly desires? What does this say about our efforts to earn God's approval?

Get the participants understand the depravity and deception of the human heart. At our core, we are stubbornly proud and bent on earning approval, yet nothing we do can earn God's approval. Good intentions and efforts can never measure up to God's perfect standards. The Pharisee proudly wore his efforts of fasting and tithing like badges of honor, but the Old Testament text (Micah) made it clear that these things could not make anyone righteous before God.

This does not mean that Christians are not called to do good works. In fact, Scripture repeatedly exhorts God's people to be "rich in good deeds" (1 Timothy 6:18), and God redeems us for the purpose of living lives of holiness and service. The key, however, is recognizing that because of the all-encompassing nature of sin, all our thoughts and actions—even our good works—are as "filthy rags," utterly useless (Isaiah 64:6). Consider a hose that has been detached from its faucet: No matter how hard it tries, it cannot spray water. Only when it is connected to a water source does it have any effectiveness at all. In the same way, we need to be connected to God, the source of life.

Jesus Completing the Story (5-10 minutes)

5. What do we learn from this parable about the necessity of Jesus' sacrifice for sin? How does his voluntary humility change our posture toward God?

The goal of this question is to understand the radical, upside-down nature of the gospel: Those who exalt themselves are humbled, but those who are humble are exalted. In Jesus' supreme example of humility and self-sacrifice (Philippians 2:6-11), we behold the Lamb of God dying for our sins. It is only in believing and accepting this humble sacrifice for sin that we are pardoned and accepted by God.

Jesus said that the tax collector went home justified before God. This meant that he no longer stood before God as a sinner, but as one who had been declared just and good by him. This can happen because Jesus, the eternal Son of God, endured the humiliation of death on the cross, through which he took on the condemnation we deserved so that we who deserve humiliation could be exalted.

Humility is not thinking less of yourself, but knowing that we need God's mercy and grace and boldly asking God for it. Humility is thinking rightly about yourself and rightly about God. When you do that, you see your need to ask for mercy, and you have the faith to ask for it.

Living Out the Story (15-20 minutes)

6. To which of the men do you more readily relate? Why?

This question should prompt deeper analysis of the ways we naturally relate to God and others.

7. What are some of the "good deeds" you rely on to earn God's favor?

This question is designed to help uncover the deceitfulness of our hearts (Jeremiah 17:9-10) and the ways we look to our own righteousness to earn God's favor.

8. How does the experience of God's graciousness and generosity to us, shown in the sacrifice of Jesus, radically alter our motivation for good deeds?

The goal of this question is to help participants understand that those who freely receive grace are empowered to freely give grace.

Additional Questions (to use if time allows)

For what is the Pharisee thankful? How does this relate to his religious practices of tithing and fasting?

The Pharisee is thankful for what he is not—robber, evildoer, adulterer, tax collector. In other words, he is thankful that he is not a person in need of mercy and forgiveness. Outwardly, he does all the right things such as tithe and fast. He seemingly does these things in order to feel superior to others and acceptable to God, rather than out of a true love for God or compassion for his neighbors.

Imagine encountering a person praying with such an outward display of shame as the tax collector. What would you think of him? What might compel a person to pray this way?

This is a highly unusual display of sorrow and expresses deep regret and self-loathing. A passerby might assume he committed some unspeakable deed that merited condemnation. The tax collector understands he is a sinner who has no reason to believe that God would accept him for anything he has done. He associates himself with those who desperately need forgiveness and mercy. He knows that God is rightfully indignant over his sin, yet he pleads for God's mercy and receives it.

What in this study has most challenged you, and why?

The goal of this question is to allow participants a time of honest sharing and community building around their own individual ideas and insights from this study.

STUDY #2
Generosity and Relationships

Luke 17:3-10
See page 13

The Text (15-20 minutes)

1. What is your response to being called an "unworthy servant," whose duty it is to offer unlimited forgiveness?

Use this first question to encourage group discussion about the Western uneasiness with master-servant relationships. Allow participants to voice their discomfort around the concept of servanthood.

2. What is the connection between Jesus' teaching on forgiveness (vv. 3-4) and his response to his disciples about faith and duty (vv. 6-10)?

Discussion should center on the connection between our debt of sin to God, which has been forgiven by Jesus, and our willingness to do our duty as fellow forgivers. The companion passage in Matthew 18:21-35, the Parable of the Unmerciful Servant, may be helpful here.

3. What are the specific steps listed in Jesus' command to forgive and how is this different from the ways we have thought of forgiveness?

Jesus outlines a specific order for forgiving others: first rebuke, then forgive, then keep forgiving! ("If your brother sins, rebuke him, and if he repents, forgive him. If he sins against you seven times in a day... forgive him" vv. 3-4). Biblical forgiveness is not simply overlooking evil or wrong. Rather, it involves pointing out the offense committed and correcting it, without demanding repayment or retribution. Imagine that a colleague wrongfully takes credit for your work on a project, injuring your reputation. Saying you forgive and yet harboring a grudge is not true forgiveness; neither is minimizing the magnitude of the offense and just letting it go. Forgiveness is difficult! In order to forgive, you must first acknowledge the extent of the wrong and the fact that someone must pay to repair the wrong, and then choose to bear the wrong yourself rather than make the other person pay the price.

This specific truth-with-grace paradigm of forgiveness requires so much more from us than we typically want to give: direct rebuke, difficult conversations, and gracious forgiveness. Jesus upends the typical standard of forgiveness by instructing us to forgive seven times a day. This isn't a literal seven times; rather, Jesus is saying that every time someone sins against us, we should forgive. In other words, we are called to forgive again and again without limit, to "forgive as the Lord forgave you" (Colossians 3:13). In other passages (such as Mark 11:25), we are commanded to forgive anyone and everyone, even those who show no signs of repentance.

The Text in the Bigger Story (5-10 minutes)

Commentators note that Jesus is referring to Leviticus 19:17-18.

4. What do you think it means to "rebuke your neighbor frankly" in the context of loving your neighbor as yourself?

This passage is calling us to speak truth in love. "Speaking truth" means that we lay aside our need to be liked and address the wrong committed so that our neighbor might change for the better. "In love" means seeking peace and reconciliation, putting our neighbor's needs and well-being above our own.

Jesus Completing the Story (5-10 minutes)

5. Jesus came "not to be served, but to serve and to give his life as a ransom for many" (Matthew 20:28). How does Jesus' life as a servant transform your understanding of what it means to forgive?

The goal of this question is to have participants contemplate the beauty of Jesus' humility and his willingness to become a servant. As master and creator of the universe, Jesus had every right to expect service and obedience from his created ones. Yet he voluntarily humbled himself to the status of a servant. In fact, since he came to serve his disciples (among others), he humbled himself to an even lower status than his own indentured servants! His example of servant humility has the power to transform our hearts, so that we can be humble, willing to rebuke, and eager to forgive.

Living Out the Story (15-20 minutes)

6. How does the forgiveness God offers us through Jesus radically transform the way we extend forgiveness to others?

Because of sin, we are infinitely indebted to God; but like many indentured servants, we have no means to earn our freedom because the debt is too enormous. No amount of human striving could erase it. It takes a wealthy person to pay off a great debt. Jesus, in whom are all riches and wealth, became poor to pay our debt, leaving the fellowship of the Trinity to become a servant in order to rescue us from the judgment we deserve (Philippians 2). Even more, his complete work of atonement has set us up with an eternal inheritance in heaven! As people whose sins have been forgiven and to whom such spiritual riches have been given, we are empowered by the gospel to extend forgiveness and seek reconciliation in even the most trying, unfair circumstances.

7. We are called to be a people of reconciliation and peace, yet we often find ourselves in situations where a lack of forgiveness has alienated us from those who have wronged us. What are some practical steps we can take to reach out to those who have sinned against us?

This is an open-ended question to encourage gospel application and group participation. Answers may range from spiritual exercises of prayer to practical steps of confronting and learning to speak the truth in love. Be prepared to share from your own personal experiences, so that others, too, will share honestly and helpfully. To the extent that your responses, as the leader, are thoughtful and helpful, so too will be the input from the group.

Additional Questions (to use if time allows)

What do you think about the disciples' response in verse 5 ("Increase our faith!")? How would you have responded?

The disciples realized that even the most religious and compassionate people of their day could not possibly live up to the standard of forgiveness that Jesus had commanded. The teaching of Judaism at the time was that three times was enough to show a forgiving spirit. If a person committed a transgression, he was forgiven the first, second, and third time, but the fourth time he was not forgiven.

The parable in verses 7-10 speaks of servants who are merely doing their duty. What might this imply about one who does not forgive?

A servant's job is to do the master's will. A servant who is unwilling to do his job implicitly views himself not as a servant, but a master. This means that when we do not forgive, we are deliberately refusing our duty as servants and are setting ourselves up as our own masters.

· In Jesus' day people who had fallen into hard times could offer themselves as indentured servants to work off their debts. These were full-time servants forced to labor around the clock until their period of servitude was over. Since this is what was expected of these servants, there would have been no reason for their master to show appreciation and serve them in return.

Think about a situation where you find it very difficult to forgive someone. How can the message of Philippians 2 foster change in you, allowing you to forgive in this challenging situation?

This is an open-ended question to encourage gospel application and honest sharing among the participants. Be prepared to share from your own personal experiences, so that others, too, will share honestly and helpfully.

STUDY #3
Hospitality and God's Grace

Luke 14:12-24
See page 19

The Text (15-20 minutes)

1. Who are the people you most like to invite to a party?

This question is intended as a conversation starter. You could also ask: "What kind of parties do you enjoy?" or "What was the last party you attended?" Use one of these questions to begin group discussion. Answers can be frivolous and fun. As the group facilitator, be prepared to provide a few answers of your own.

2. In verses 15-24, two different groups of people are invited to a great banquet at two different times. How would you describe the first group that was invited to the banquet?

They had the means to decline an invitation to such a lavish banquet. They were successful and well regarded. Typically, only the social elite would be invited to such an event. They were self-sufficient. These were networking events, and their refusal to come revealed that they felt no need to be in relationship with the host.

3. How would you describe the second group that was invited to the banquet?

They were poor, crippled, blind, and lame. These people were suffering, needy, and completely dependent on the help of others. They had nothing to offer the host and were therefore unlikely guests. They were outcasts of society. These were the people who had no social capital or networking connections, and thus were easily overlooked.

The Text in the Bigger Story (5-10 minutes)

Jesus' contemporaries would have been reminded of the future kingdom banquet of Isaiah 25:6-9.

4. How would you describe the Isaiah feast, and what does this tell you about God and his kingdom?

The goal of this question is to explore the lavishness of God's generosity and get a glimpse of his future kingdom. The feast in Isaiah is described as:

- Extravagant: There is enough for "all peoples"—a bountiful feast indeed! The invitation is broad.
- Highest quality: The words that describe the feast are rich and best and finest. This is a picture of heaven and the riches of God's kingdom.
- Celebratory: Suffering and death will be forever destroyed. Tears will be wiped away, and disgrace and shame will have no place. In response, God's people will joyfully proclaim the wonders of his grace.

We learn that God abounds in love and gracious provision! God promises an eternal kingdom of abundance, joy, and celebration. God triumphs over sin, destruction, death, and shame. God's kingdom is a place of wholeness and healing. There will no longer be any suffering.

Jesus Completing the Story (5-10 minutes)

5. What do you learn from this parable about the heart and intention of God?

God's one great desire is for fellowship with his created people. His love and generous commitment to us is so immense and unconditional that he made a way for reconciliation, in order that we may join his eternal kingdom banquet!

Living Out the Story (15-20 minutes)

6. Who are the people on the margins of the Luke banquet? And who are the people on the margins of our invitation lists?

Have your group consider practical ways of reaching beyond your typical comfort zones or affinity groups in order to express the generosity of Jesus to marginalized groups. First consider who these people are. In the following question, you will consider practical ways to make room for outsiders in your lives and spheres of influence.

7. The Greek word for hospitality is *philoxenia,* which literally means "love of strangers." What are some ways that we can make room for those who are not typical "party invitees," those who are unwelcomed and excluded in our society?

Have participants consider practical ways of reaching beyond our typical comfort zones or affinity groups, in order to express the generosity of Jesus to marginalized groups in our neighborhoods. As the leader, be prepared with specific ideas and examples. You may want to propose a group service project that addresses the ideas presented by the group.

Additional Questions (to use if time allows)

What is your opinion about the excuses used by the first set of guests? Are they legitimate?

Work, possessions, and relationships usually make fine excuses to skip out on a party. But Jesus was highlighting the importance of prioritizing these things relative to the type of invitation given. There is no excuse to turn down the invitation to dine at the table in God's kingdom (v. 15).

It was a great honor to be invited to such a banquet, so the refusal to participate communicated to the host: "I have no need of you. This is not important or worth my time." This was a slap in the face. The guests who did come to the party made no excuses, but rather eagerly received the generosity of the host.

Jesus became poor so that we might become rich (2 Corinthians 8:9). What are some ways you have experienced his generosity and love?

We have been blessed with every spiritual blessing:
- Eternal life. We have been "adopted as his sons through Jesus Christ" (Ephesians 1:5).
- Redemption and the forgiveness of our sins (Ephesians 1:7).
- Lavish wisdom and understanding (Ephesians 1:8).
- New identity. We are God's children and heirs of God (Romans 8:17). As sons and daughters of our Heavenly Father, we have full access to God and a right to all the privileges of being part of his family.

- Holy Spirit. The Holy Spirit gives us new life by making us more and more like Jesus. He is our comforter (John 14), counselor, and conduit of God's truth and wisdom.

How does the experience of God's hospitality change your heart about giving with the expectation of receiving something in return?

God's grace is completely free and totally undeserved! We don't live the perfect holy life that we should, but yet God regards us as those who do. This is what is meant by our being "in Christ" (Ephesians 1). God sees us as in the same position of his Son! The experience of God's love for us changes us. Since God extended grace to us while we were his enemies, we are called to be generous to those who don't deserve it.

STUDY #4

Generosity and Ministry

Luke 9:49-10:2
See page 25

The Text (15-20 minutes)

1. Before sending his followers out to serve others, Jesus first clears up misconceptions about what it means to follow him. What are some modern-day misconceptions you have heard about what it means to follow Jesus?

Use this question as a conversation ice breaker to warm up group discussion. As the group facilitator, be prepared to provide a few answers of your own, such as the misconception of political party affiliation, prohibitions on dancing or drinking or contraceptive use, requirement of regular church attendance and tithing, etc.

2. What were the misconceptions of Jesus' listeners (vv. 49-62)?

Jesus was addressing his followers, who thought
- they were inherently better because of their disciple status (v.49),
- they deserved to judge those who didn't accept Jesus (v. 54), and
- that following Jesus is simple and doesn't require self-sacrifice (v. 57).

3. What do you learn from Jesus' response?

The goal of this question is to see that following Jesus means aligning our desires with his kingdom purposes and to unveil our misconceptions of what it means to follow Jesus.

Jesus rebukes his disciples for their error of thinking themselves superior to others. The disciples felt that they were part of an exclusive group, because Jesus personally chose them, and thus, how dare this outsider perform miracles in Jesus' name! They missed the point, however, failing to see that Jesus choosing them was an act of pure grace and not in response to their worthiness. Similarly, as Jesus' followers, we must not miss this important truth! We should have postures of humility that result from understanding God's grace. We ought to beware of a similar tendency to pride and self-exaltation, remembering that we are called to follow Jesus in lives of self-sacrifice.

The Text in the Bigger Story (5-10 minutes)

In 2 Corinthians 5:17-20, the Apostle Paul further unpacks this idea that Jesus' followers are sent out into the world to serve.

4. What are the primary responsibilities of an ambassador, and what should be our responsibilities as "Christ's ambassadors"?

The goal of this question is to understand that Jesus' mission is one of reconciliation. The primary responsibilities of an ambassador are to represent and embody the qualities of the sending party, to promote peace and goodwill to a foreign delegation.

As Christ reconciled us to God, we are called to share this message of reconciliation to all people. Therefore, we are his messengers and representatives to others. We are Christ's presence to the world. Furthermore, since our message is about God showing love to us, it is essential that we demonstrate that same love to others. It is not sufficient to merely speak of Jesus; people must see a Jesus likeness in us.

5. What are some challenges to our roles as Christ's ambassadors?

There are several challenges to consider, among which are the following:

Ourselves: the temptation to promote our own agendas over the message of reconciliation.

Excluding others: the temptation to surround ourselves with like-minded "citizens" rather than "foreigners." If we understand the gospel to be a message of reconciliation, how can we exclude others?

Jesus Completing the Story (5-10 minutes)

6. What about Jesus' life and death helps us understand his rebuke in verses 49-62?

Just as Jesus gave all of himself to reconcile us to God, we likewise must embody a deep spirit of generosity to serve as his presence to the world. Jesus came to earth to save sinners. He did not come in a half-hearted, halfway attempt at reconciliation. His self-sacrifice was complete in every way: bodily (born a baby; became a man) and emotionally (lived among sin and sorrow, a suffering servant called the "man of sorrows") and relationally (forsaken by his Father).

Living Out the Story (15-20 minutes)

7. In verse 2 Jesus tells his followers that "the harvest is plentiful, but the workers are few." In what areas of your community or neighborhood do you see plentiful needs with few workers?

Have your group explore ways in which we can practically serve those in our communities. Be prepared to list places of need in your specific neighborhood and encourage your group to think creatively about ways to address the needs.

8. What prejudices do we harbor in our own hearts and what steps can we take to seek reconciliation?

The goal of this question is to acknowledge that we, like Jesus' disciples (vv. 49-56), likely harbor deep-seated prejudices of which we are unaware. It is likely that we are blind to the favoritism we show to those who are like us in education, status, class, or race.

Additional Questions (to use if time allows)

How would you describe the disciples' reaction to the Samaritans (vv. 51-56)? What do you think is the motive behind their actions?

Whereas the disciples exclude the first man on the basis of his not being part of their group, the disciples reject the Samaritans on the basis of their opposition to Jesus. Beneath the surface, the disciples had contempt and disdain toward Samaritans, who were considered traitors because their Jewish ancestors intermarried with neighboring nations. Jews and Samaritans were enemies, and the disciples' reaction reveals a spirit of animosity and racial superiority. Jesus refuses to condemn the Samaritans because his message was one of peace and reconciliation. He demonstrates to his disciples that they must be gracious even to those who oppose them and those they dislike.

What is your reaction to the rather harsh-sounding words of Jesus to potential followers (vv.57- 62)?

First, allow participants to voice their objections or surprise. Then, discuss using the following prompts:

- Housing issues and family obligations are certainly valid concerns. The point is not that Jesus' followers must neglect these things, but that the kingdom of God takes precedence over even the things we regard as most important.
- Their primary identity is that they are members of the kingdom. Anyone who cannot accept this is not ready to follow him. In the previous verses, he says, "If anyone would come after me, he must deny himself and take up his cross daily and follow me. For whoever wants to save his life will lose it, but whoever loses his life for me will save it. What good is it for a man to gain the whole world, and yet lose or forfeit his very self?" (Luke 9:23-25). You cannot follow Jesus halfway.

How does Jesus' sacrifice show us how we are to relate to those who are not in the "inner circle" or those who oppose us?

God's message of reconciliation is for all people, particularly the outsider. Much of Jesus' earthly ministry focused on outsiders: tax collectors, the Samaritan woman, lepers, etc. Jesus left his heavenly glory to live among us, providing us the ultimate example of sacrificial service and generosity. He instructs us to likewise extend grace and generosity to those outside our comfort zones. As he was dying on the cross, Jesus prayed, "Father, forgive them, for they do not know what they are doing" (Luke 23:34). Just as Jesus prayed for his enemies even as they crucified him, we should extend forgiveness and grace to those who oppose us.

Verses 57-62 list some things that tend to take precedence over serving God and others. Take a minute to assemble your own mental list of competing desires or conflicting priorities. What can we do to protect ourselves from being consumed by life's demands?

This is an open-ended question to encourage honest sharing and practical application. Be prepared to share from your own personal experiences, so that others, too, will share honestly and helpfully.

STUDY #5

Generosity and Wealth, Part 1

Luke 18:18-30
See page 31

The Text (15-20 minutes)

1. What are the possessions you hold most dear?

Use this question as a conversation starter to warm up group discussion. As the group facilitator, be prepared to share your own answer. Answers could be something like the following: family photo albums, retirement portfolio, heirloom, jewelry, antique watch, a long-lasting friendship, etc.

2. The rich ruler claimed that he had faithfully kept all the commandments since his youth. Why then was it so difficult for him to follow Jesus' command in verse 22?

Following Jesus means much more than external obedience and requires that we trust in him more than in other things. The things that naturally keep us from God are accentuated by wealth, which is why Jesus repeatedly addressed the dangers of wealth. In Luke 12:15 he says, "Watch out! Be on your guard against all kinds of greed."

3. Is Jesus' command to sell everything and give to the poor required of everyone who seeks to follow him? Why or why not?

While there is nothing inherently evil about wealth, it exerts enormous power over us in insidious ways. Jesus spoke about money and the dangers of wealth on many occasions, warning about the "deceitfulness of wealth" (Matthew 13:22). Wealth deceives by lulling us into a false sense of security, by creating an unending desire for more, and by replacing our primary need of repentance with proud independence.

In no other instance in the gospels does Jesus command someone to give away all they have. For example, when sought out by the affluent Jewish council member, Nicodemus, Jesus mentioned nothing about money (John 3). The point is not a one-size-fits-all mandate, but rather an important principle about wealth and possessions.

4. What are some of the things in which we place our trust and security? And why are these things such spiritual traps?

We turn God's good gifts of wealth and success into ultimate things that we think will bring security and self-worth. This is one reason that we always feel like we need just a little more, because what we have never satisfies the true longing of our hearts.

The Text in the Bigger Story (5-10 minutes)

The rich ruler thought he had done everything he was required to do because he kept the Ten Commandments. In Deuteronomy 10:12-15, however, God showed his people what true obedience meant.

5. According to this passage, what was lacking about the rich ruler's obedience?

His obedience was a means to an end. While the commandments were given by God to address the hearts and motivations of his people, the rich ruler had turned them into an exercise of moralistic one-upmanship. His true trust was in his wealth, thereby breaking the first commandment to "have no other gods before me." Essentially, he was saying that he would rather serve created things (his wealth) than the Creator. But created things were only meant to be gifts from God, not gods themselves. We either love and serve God, or we love and serve something else.

Jesus Completing the Story (5-10 minutes)

6. Jesus says that no one who has forsaken family or riches to follow him "will fail to receive many times as much in this age and, in the age to come, eternal life." What are some things we find in Jesus that our idols cannot provide?

The goal of this question is to acknowledge that God's provision and generosity are infinitely greater than anything we can earn ourselves. Although the group may have additional insights, following is a list of the treasures given by God:

Permanence and security. No matter how secure the investment, material wealth is always at risk; it is always "uncertain" (1 Timothy 6:17). Thus, the pursuit of financial security leaves us always looking for more. It is subject to so many factors that are beyond our control, and eventually it fades away. Our days are limited, and someday we will leave behind our material possessions. Jesus, however, offers eternal life and a secure future to all who follow him.

Purpose and community. In the book of Acts, we see that Christians treated their possessions as if they belonged to God and should be used to serve others. When Jesus makes us a part of this kind of community, our possessions and gifts can be used to bless others, providing a sense of purpose as well as a strengthened community.

Peace and rest. We can diligently strive to achieve wealth, status, power, and influence, but even when we attain it, we find these things fail to fully satisfy us. In Jesus we find the source of eternal rest (Hebrews 4) that allows us to cease from our many strivings. Jesus calls us to come to him for rest (Matthew 11:28), and in him we find the true satisfaction of all our longings.

Living Out the Story (15-20 minutes)

7. What would it look like to faithfully serve God with our wealth and all he has given us? What area of your life would be most affected?

Explore how God's generosity toward us in Christ enables us to use everything he has given us to serve him and others. Be prepared to personally address the ways your life would be affected, and then encourage your group to consider practical, concrete ways their lives would be most affected by applying this lesson.

Additional Questions (to use if time allows)

If this command was not meant for everyone, why do you think Jesus required it of the young ruler?

Since not all people are called to sell everything, Jesus must be addressing something that has particular power over the rich ruler's heart. In a way, observing the commands in verse 20 was relatively easy; following Jesus' was not. A very rich man like him had so much to lose in following Christ.

The passage does not indicate that the rich ruler was particularly greedy or excessively self-indulgent. Neither is there any indication that he attained his wealth through illicit means. It is clear, however, that his material wealth was more important to him than even eternal life. In other words, his wealth was his idol—the thing he worshiped as most valuable in his life. In Luke 16:13 Jesus teaches that we cannot serve both God and money. To follow Jesus, the rich ruler had to give up what was most important to him, his great wealth. With great sadness, he left for home unchanged by Jesus' words.

What does God require of his people (vv. 12-13)?

God requires that we serve him with all our heart, soul, mind, and strength. Keeping the commandment is meant to be a wholehearted response to experiencing his abundant love for us.

What are some of the reasons we should walk in God's ways and love and serve him?

We should do these things for our own good (v. 13). God's laws teach us how we can live the most joyful and fulfilling lives. Conversely, when we stray from God's commands, we bring injury and sorrow upon ourselves. We should be moved to obey because of his exceedingly great love for us (vv. 14-15). God holds all the universe in his hands, yet he chose his people to love because it pleased him to do so. Walking in his ways and loving and serving God should be an overflow of a heart touched by his grace.

In what ways do we make our wealth and material things more important than they actually are?

This is an open-ended question meant to prompt deeper understanding of our core motivations, as well as to encourage honest sharing among the participants. Be prepared to share from your own personal experiences, so that others, too, will share honestly and helpfully.

STUDY # 6
Generosity and Wealth, Part 2

Luke 16:1-14
See page 37

The Text (15-20 minutes)

1. Why do you think Jesus would use this example to teach his disciples how to make friends?

This is an open-ended question, meant to prompt speculation and deeper group engagement with the text. One consideration is to understand Jesus' emphasis on our relationships with others, and the value of people above possessions.

2. What is surprising about the way in which the manager secured his future (vv. 3-7)?

He was dishonest (v. 8). It is not clear why Jesus labels him as such, but two possible explanations are: 1) that he may have initially charged exorbitant interest to his master's debtors and kept a portion for himself, or 2) that by discounting the loans, he cheated his master in order to ingratiate himself with potential employers. In either case, he acted out of selfish motives. Although the end result was positive for others (the debtors must have been elated to suddenly owe significantly less), it was motivated by the manager's self interests.

3. What is Jesus teaching his followers about wealth and relationships?

In telling a story of how a "person of this world" acted wisely, Jesus implies that his followers, being people of God's kingdom, should behave even more shrewdly. If "people of this world" know how to shrewdly use their wealth to make friends, how much more should Christians, who have experienced unlimited riches in Jesus, use their wealth to welcome others into God's family. If this manager could see that relationships are more important than wealth, how much more so for Christians who ought to consider their relationship to Jesus their greatest treasure.

The Text in the Bigger Story (5-10 minutes)

In 1 Chronicles 29:12-16, King David praises God for his provision of materials to build God's temple.

4. Compare King David and the manager in Luke, particularly their attitudes about wealth. What does King David's prayer teach us about how we should view wealth?

The goal of this question is to understand that everything we have belongs to God and that we are called to be wise stewards of the wealth he gives us to serve him. Since King David understood that all his wealth came from God (v. 12), he saw himself as merely a manager of God's resources. Like the manager in Luke, David was free to use his wealth as he saw fit, but he acknowledged that he was to ultimately give an account to his Master. Just as the manager realized that he would be ruined without the benevolence of a wealthy master, David understood that he would be nothing without God's generosity (vv. 14-15). He accurately understood that his wealth was the confluence of many factors outside of his control—health, talent, abilities, and opportunities—none of which David took for granted. So when he prayed, "Everything comes from you, and we have given you only what comes from your hand," he was appropriately acknowledging God as the source of all his wealth.

Jesus Completing the Story (5-10 minutes)

5. What "true riches" (v. 11) does Jesus give us that worldly wealth cannot?

True riches come from experiencing the love of Christ, who laid aside his heavenly riches to provide us with lasting treasure and community. Money is "a shelter" but can only offer us temporary security and comfort. After a while, the benefits of our current level of wealth fade and we need to spend more to get more. Jesus, however, offers lasting peace and eternal security without us having to earn it. King Solomon, the Bible's example of ultimate wealth and security, wrote about the inferior shelter of money: "Wisdom is a shelter as money is a shelter, but the advantage of knowledge is this: Wisdom preserves those who have it" (Ecclesiastes 7:12).

Money itself is temporary. No matter how much you have, someday you will have to part with it. But Jesus promises that he will be with us forever. Money does not have the capacity to care about or love you. But God's love for us is evident in the gift of his son Jesus, who he sent that we might enter into joyful, eternal fellowship with him.

Living Out the Story (15-20 minutes)

6. Share with the group some ways you have experienced God's riches this week. How can we use our wealth (and other resources) to build relationships that welcome others into God's kingdom?

This is an open-ended question meant to prompt deeper understanding of the material, as well as to encourage honest sharing among the group. Be prepared to share from your own personal experiences, so that others, too, will share honestly and helpfully.

7. What are some ways we can be more generous with our money? In particular, consider how we can limit some of our spending so we can be more flexible in our giving.

This is an open-ended question meant to explore the practical implications of Jesus' teaching with regard to wise, kingdom-centered stewardship. As the group leader, be prepared to share from your own personal experiences, so that others, too, will share on a deeper level.

Additional Questions (to use if time allows)

How were the manager's actions commendable and effective?

A less shrewd man may have accepted his fate as a beggar or manual laborer, but the manager craftily (and wisely) used his master's wealth to secure future employment. He was very strategic. He gave up short-term financial profit to make friends. This manager, who spent his master's wealth lavishly and irresponsibly (v. 1), nevertheless understood that relationships, not money, would save him from financial and social disaster. He used his shrewdness to secure his future and build beneficial relationships.

The manager was able to "buy" his friends. How is this different from the community we experience through Jesus?

The debtors were pleased with the manager only because he offered financial benefits. Without this, they would have no reason to befriend him. Christian community, however, is not self-serving; it seeks to imitate Jesus, who out of love, gave all of himself to serve others. Furthermore, since Jesus often associated with the outcasts of society, Christian community welcomes even those who can offer no apparent benefit. The bond between Jesus' followers is based on Christ's sacrificial love for them, not on a cost-benefit analysis.

How can we as a group hold each other accountable for being good stewards and managers of the money God has given us?

This is an open-ended question meant to explore the practical implications of Jesus' teaching with regard to wise, kingdom-centered stewardship. As the group leader, be prepared to contribute ideas that are tailored to your participants.

STUDY #7

Generosity and Power

Luke 19:1-9
See page 43

The Text

1. What are some things we tend to value most in life? How have we, like Zacchaeus, "sold out" to our careers or other cultural values?

Use this question as a conversation starter to warm up group discussion. As the group facilitator, be prepared to share your own answer. Answers could be along the lines of workaholic tendencies, financial security, overvaluing our children, seeking validation from personal accomplishments or alliances, etc.

2. What are the differences between Zacchaeus before and after his encounter with Jesus?

The goal of this question is to consider the radical transformation of Zacchaeus after meeting Jesus. Before encountering Jesus, Zacchaeus was a chief tax collector with a bad reputation. As a chief tax collector working for a foreign government, Zacchaeus would have been considered a traitor and a mercenary. Tax collectors often dealt unscrupulously with taxpayers, collecting considerably more than was required and keeping the difference. It seems that Zacchaeus, in spite of the outward animosity he would incur, was willing to be considered a traitor because of his love of money.

After his encounter with Jesus, however, Zacchaeus immediately became a generous man and cannot seem to get rid of his money quickly enough—half of his possessions to the poor and repayment of all money he gained by cheating people. In verse 8, Zacchaeus said, "If I have cheated anybody out of anything, I will pay back four times the amount." In the Old Testament, the most severe penalty for fraudulent crimes was repayment of four times the stolen amount. Zacchaeus voluntarily applied the most severe economic penalty to himself. His encounter with Jesus had a powerful impact on the way he now lived his life. In Luke 16:13, Jesus said: "You cannot serve both God and money. Either you will hate the one and love the other, or you will be devoted to one and despise the other." The change we see in Zacchaeus is that although he once loved money and despised God, the situation was reversed after meeting Jesus.

The Text in the Bigger Story (5-10 minutes)

The apostle Paul, like Zacchaeus, experienced a life-transforming encounter with Jesus and wrote about it in Philippians 3:7-8, 13-14.

3. How are Paul and Zacchaeus able to joyfully let go of things that used to be so important to them?

The goal of this question is to understand that in Jesus' acceptance of us we receive all-surpassing joy and a new identity. These changes are "everything we need for life and godliness," empowering dynamic changes in our lives and loosening the grip of former claims and affections. In order for anyone to loosen their grip on something they value, they must first find something else of surpassing worth, a greater affection to replace a lesser one. For Paul and Zacchaeus, "knowing Christ Jesus" (v. 8), or in other words, being in relationship with him, provided them with greater joy and profit than anything else could. Jesus replaced the position that money had occupied in Zacchaeus' life. Jesus replaced the position that power and religious performance had occupied in Paul's life.

4. What were the most obvious changes in Zacchaeus' (and Paul's) relationships to God after encountering Jesus?

The most obvious and immediate changes were joy and a new identity. Although Zacchaeus was labeled a "sinner" by everyone in his community, Jesus loved and accepted him. This unconditional acceptance radically altered his identity from one of societal scorn to security and acceptance. Like Zacchaeus, Paul was the object of contempt and fear. He was a terrorist who fearlessly persecuted Christians! After his encounter with Jesus, however, he was able to forget what was in his past (his despised reputation) and embrace his new calling. God's grace and forgiveness empowered complete transformations!

Zacchaeus was called a "son of Abraham" (v. 9) by Jesus and was welcomed into God's family. Paul was called to be an apostle of Jesus, where once he had been an enemy of the church. In his letters to Christian churches, Paul repeatedly labeled himself an apostle and servant of Jesus Christ, not mentioning that he formerly abused Christ-followers. It's as if he was completely freed of his former reputation. Able to rejoice in their new identities, both Paul and Zacchaeus discovered power to fulfill their new callings.

Jesus Completing the Story (5-10 minutes)

5. Jesus makes a remarkable statement in verse 9 that applies to all who receive him. What does it mean for a "sinner" like Zacchaeus to become a "son of Abraham"?

The lavish grace of Jesus provides unexpected and astounding results! Even those far off from God, not keeping his laws, not accepted by the religious followers, are called into the covenant of God that originated with Abraham. To be called "a son of Abraham" equated the "sinner" Zacchaeus with all those who had kept God's laws.

Living Out the Story (15-20 minutes)

6. The gospel changes everything about our lives, from our most notable strengths to our innermost motives. Can you think of subtle ways in which you wield power or influence? What would it look like to have a Zacchaeus-like transformation in your sphere of influence?

Consider how our areas of influence (work, home, family, church, government, neighborhood, etc.) might look different if transformed by the presence of Jesus "showing up at our house." As the group leader, be prepared to share your own example and/or to explore practical ways you and your group members can respond to the gospel in the areas of power and influence.

7. Zacchaeus expressed delight and satisfaction in giving away his wealth. Have you experienced a similar joy in giving away power, status, possessions, or wealth?

The goal of this question is to prompt deeper sharing and perhaps a recent testimony of how this Generosity study has stimulated new changes in the lives of your group members. As the group leader, be prepared to share honestly from your own life. Consider the full implications of a posture of generosity, not just with money but also with one's time, talents, and hospitality. Consider how the gospel informs so much more than our own definitions of generosity.

Use this final question to address the important lessons you've learned by exploring the implications of gospel generosity in these seven lessons.

Additional Questions (to use if time allows)

What does Jesus mean by his statement: "Today salvation has come to this house" (v. 9)?

On the surface, it looks like Jesus is just now saying that Zacchaeus has been saved. After all, it is evident from his actions that Zacchaeus has undergone a profound change. However, Jesus is not saying that Zacchaeus was saved as a result of giving his wealth away. He is saying, "I am salvation. You are not saved by anything you do. You are saved by what I do, and by what I am going to do."

It is only through Jesus' life, death, and resurrection that we can be reconciled to God. Our best deeds—even the recompense shown by Zacchaeus and outlined in Moses' Law—do not earn our salvation. The only way a sinner like Zacchaeus could receive salvation was for Jesus to graciously and lovingly enter his life. Only after Jesus went to Zacchaeus' home did Zacchaeus give away his wealth; his actions were a response to the good news.

What in this study has challenged you the most, and why? What has encouraged you the most, and why?

The goal of this question is to prompt deeper sharing and perhaps a recent testimony of how this lesson has stimulated new changes in the lives of your group members. As the group leader, be prepared to share honestly from your own life.